YOUR

WORLD...

AND WELCOME TO IT

Also by Patrick Mauriès
CHRISTIAN LACROIX: THE DIARY OF A COLLECTION

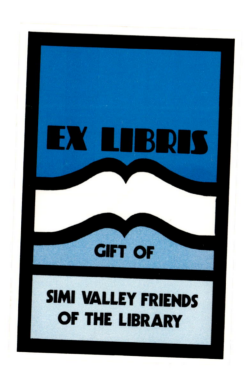

SIMON & SCHUSTER EDITIONS

YOUR WORLD...
AND WELCOME TO IT

A Rogue's Gallery of Interior Design

TEXT BY
PATRICK MAURIÈS

ILLUSTRATIONS BY
CHRISTIAN LACROIX

TRANSLATION BY CHRISTOPHER PHILLIPS

For Françoise De Nobele,
Jacques Leguennec,
and Alain Ozanne

Simon & Schuster Editions
Rockefeller Center
1230 Avenue of the Americas
New York, NY 10020

Published by arrangement with Éditions Gallimard

SIMON & SCHUSTER EDITIONS and colophon are trademarks of Simon & Schuster Inc.

Designed by Tika Buchanan, Eric Baker Design Associates

Manufactured in the United States of America

10 9 8 7 6 5 4 3 2 1

Library of Congress Cataloging-in-Publication Data

Mauriès, Patrick, date.
    [Styles d'aujourd'hui. English]
    Your world—and welcome to it: a rogue's gallery of interior
    design / written by Patrick Mauriès; illustrations by Christian Lacroix;
    translation by Christopher Phillips.
       p. cm.
    1. Interior decoration—History—20th century—Themes, motives.
    2. Interior decoration—History—20th century—Caricatures and cartoons.
    3. French wit and humor, Pictorial. I. Lacroix, Christian, date. II. Title.
NK1980.M3413 1998
747'.09 ' 04—dc21
                                     98-6317
                                     CIP

ISBN 0-684-84420-6

Contents

PREFACE

Putting first things first, I bow to the memory of the magnificent Sir Osbert Lancaster. He was a caricaturist and also something of a caricature himself, with his bushy eyebrows, thick mustache, deadpan face under a bowler hat, gentlemanly manners, and a knighthood to boot. All these things worked together to make him the eternal, or at least archetypal, Englishman.

In his writings and his drawings he unleashed the fictional Lady Littlehampton (Maudie to her intimates) upon the world's consciousness, and especially her hair-raising decorating exploits in her newly inherited stately home, Drayneflete. English people of the genuine old school, who are themselves a precious but dwindling natural resource, cherish his memory.

Across the Channel, the late Philippe Jullian, the writer, illustrator, arbiter of style, and genuine Anglophile, was not blind to Sir Osbert's gifts. A rotund man with a reserve and self-control of truly Britannic proportions, Philippe Jullian turned his spidery hand to creating subtle impressions of his own, populated by angular characters. His books show the warm spot in his heart for architecture as a mirror of history, but he added a touch of Proustian sociology and his considerable connoisseurship of the highways and byways of snobbishness.

His book *Les Styles,* which he published in 1961, became in its way what we would call a cult classic—an English phrase that has even made its way into French but doesn't properly convey the deathless appeal of certain books that, once finished, are still revered for their broken bindings and dog-eared pages and for the indelible imprint they make on sensitive souls. The liveliness, the just-rightness of tone, and the admirable bite with which his sketches delineated changes in taste in arbitrary five-year increments have more than earned the secret but tenacious devotion that the sight of this book's distinctive blue-and-yellow dust jacket can still inspire.

Sir Osbert Lancaster benefited from the natural interest in creature comforts and decorating flair among certain segments of the Anglo-Saxon public of his day. And Philippe Jullian occupied a similar position in France for the thoroughbred readers of full-color magazines like *Plaisir de France* and *Connaissance des Arts*.

More than three decades have passed since the books by these two men had their heyday. The pages have yellowed. The ground rules have changed. The world of style has been enriched and enlivened by innumerable variations and innovations. And the last few years have seen a marked acceleration in the speed and force of those changes. The explanation for this new and dizzying pace can be found among the baby boomers, who were born at the crest of the century and whose formative years were partly formed by the works of Philippe Jullian.

The baby boomers were the ones who, in the 1960s, amid the full flowering of the culture of narcissism, gave the fashion magazines a new lease on life. Every month saw fresh ones springing up, often from Italy, swollen with the excess weight of color advertisements and bursting with a seemingly limitless number of images of beauty.

In the end, the fashion magazines became tiresome. Dressed-up homes started to supplant dressed-up people as the subject of choice. Smelling fresh meat, the pundits went on the alert. Sociologists and trend oracles with astonishing names like Faith Popcorn began to prophesy a new mood of withdrawal, the end of frippery, the devotion to home and armchair, the descent into cocooning. And the baby boomers, doing what they were told, began rushing in their demographically bulging hordes to try to find themselves between the glossy covers of the shelter magazines, the new dream books.

What they found there—and all too often swallowed whole—was a fashion parade, which the authors, baby boomers themselves, wish to memorialize here in this very personal album.

I n the 1960s, Horizontal Modern was radical chic as far as decoration was concerned.

The Modern Horizontals were obsessed with volumes, space, and pure lines. Sober elegance was on their minds and little enough mercy was in their hearts as they attacked the ceilings of their apartments to purify them of their ornamental icing and other decorative conceits. Then they carved their rooms into "zones": the hearth, the bar, the open-plan kitchen (later, the kitchenette). Walls were clad in brick, pebbles, or slate—materials prized for their primitive, natural, and tactile qualities; grainy stucco was another favorite because of its texture. Finnish rugs were scattered on tile or flagstone floors that were heated from below.

This particular take on contemporary elegance originated in the north, in regions whose very flatness more or less screamed, "tabula rasa." A teak coffee table and matching armchairs were de rigueur; light-toned leather or cowhide echoed the inevitable abstract painting that dominated the room.

At least one wall celebrated the cult of the horizontal— that is to say there was a great expanse of flexible shelving units (always of teak or rosewood) proudly displaying the TV set, a collection of *Reader's Digest* books, family photos, holiday souvenirs, and a record player.

The Modern Horizontals also had their icons: chairs by Bertoia, Eames, Le Corbusier, or Mies; the Knoll table; the Aalto vase; Fornasetti plates; Gio Ponti glassware. Gleaming glass from Italy or somewhere in Scandinavia was also greatly prized. The beams of light glancing off them (sensual, yes, but oh, so abstract) were redeeming relics of a bibelotmania that was their secret shame.

In a watered-down form, Horizontal Modern set the tone for the interiors of our childhoods: splay-legged tables with polyurethane-coated tops, hard straight-backed chairs, kidney-shaped this's and thats, sofas covered in synthetics with exotic names like Leatherette and Cordual. Topping it all off as the living room's chief bourgeois appointment was that puny descendant of the imposing hutches of days gone by—a low sideboard topped with a nest of doilies and glass ornaments under a Venetian wall mirror.

Horizontal Modern, which the Italians have dignified with the name *Modernariato*, has been preserved in amber in certain boutiques, which are treasure houses of unconscious nostalgia. You can't miss them: Just look for the word *Scandinavian* in the name.

Horizontal Modern

SETTING THE TONE FOR THE INTERIORS OF OUR CHILDHOODS.

**I**n a way it was too good to be true that France's most reverently correct design firm, the House of Jansen, should have shared a name with a seventeenth-century religious reform movement that was the closest a Catholic country can come to Puritanism.

For if ever there were fierce guardians of the Great Tradition in French decorative style, they were these latter-day Jansenists, who honored and burnished each of its formulas like a verse of holy writ. Among these discreet, understated (though incredibly swanky) esthetes of the Dior- and Chanel- wearing classes, God was indeed in the details. Convinced of the importance of their mission and of their own personal contributions to it (beliefs, if the truth be told, that are fiercely held by every decorator on earth), they chose the path of learned intransigence, of sensual austerity.

And in truth it was masterful the way they combined pearl gray and bright yellow, myrtle green and cornflower blue, amaranth red and cypress

They chose the path of learned intransigence, of sensual austerity.

green: Velvet and heavy ribbed silk, draperies of striped faille and cerise pekin silk constituted their everyday fare. "One of the secrets of Georges Geffroy," the magazine *Plaisir de France* reported blandly about one of the Jansen designers, "is without a doubt using old techniques to express the taste of today. Here, plain white tailor's backing reminds one of the wool satin of another era, which was dethroned by chintz and percale."

Like the Colefaxes and Fowlers of a slightly later period, the decorative Jansenists loved furniture dating from transitional periods—hybrids or fluid mixtures that didn't fall exactly into one stylistic school or another and were all the more admired for it. The period 1780 to 1830 was the perfect place to trawl for specimens. Jansen interiors did not make much use of sofas, which are unconscionable when there are straight-back late Louis XVI or Louis XVII banquettes available; rather than corner divans, they favored Roman-style curve-legged stools, which at least kept one's posture up to the mark.

Good sports in spite of everything, the Jansenists lightened their severity with playful touches: They had a penchant for trompe l'oeil as a way to add spice to life. They were also good at livening up the most prosaic sideboard with a scattering of nineteenth-century picture frames or a display box of butterflies, and knew just when to grace doors and walls, cupboards and wardrobes with little jokes of perspective and witty columns of gray porphyry.

In short, the House of Jansen indulged a nostalgia for a time when people didn't have to measure everything down to the last inch or worry about finding enough room to store their shirts.

A *salonnière* along the lines of Madame du Deffand two centuries before her (with the important difference that she lavished her attentions on interior decoration instead of on Sir Horace Walpole), Madeleine Castaing passed her afternoons for almost half a century ensconced in an armchair on the corner of the rue Jacob and the rue Bonaparte. There she received well-dressed young men, society ladies, and high-strung esthetes.

A doll-like, totemic figure, the unquestionable gold standard in a world where one lapse in taste could do you in, she would sit there like an oracle and sometimes reveal a few prices to those clients who were bold enough to inquire. The prices, incidentally, were as changeable and unpredictable as a stock market ticker in the middle of a monetary crisis. But still, her coded messages were granted like gifts of grace in the strictest of sects. Mind-boggling as those prices could be, her delivery was the fruit of long experience (or careful strategy?) that occasionally mixed in a little histrionics. Overflowing lipstick and long false eyelashes were Madame Castaing's personal trademarks: If she sometimes stooped to little-girl cuteness, at least she could pull it off.

One visited her domain with reverence. Cracked, fissured, patched, but maintained in its original state with a rare sense of rigor, it was in a way an exact reflection of its owner. Innumerable lady editors found themselves bowled over by the tempera-painted walls in "Castaing green," the roundels, and the Greek and palmette friezes all loaded with 1947-vintage dust. The details of this interior, imperfections and all, were copied meticulously just as they had been executed according to the exacting dictates of Madame Castaing's fantasy: bare upholstery wadding nailed on the walls, chairs in need of re-covering, faded dustcovers, frayed carpeting, gloomy curtains with large Persian flower patterns, wall panels of pekin silk.

Biedermeier, Regency, and Russian styles vied for attention, along with mahogany, creamware, alabaster, and Karelian birch. Mystifying little bits of furniture, including faux-bamboo chairs made more for looking at than anything else, punctuated the space. Daring prints cheered things up: panther patterns on sofas, banana leaves or bright-colored roses on carpets. The little gaming tables adrift in a sea of plaid gave the place a certain world-weariness.

Madeleine Castaing was not one to eschew the avant-garde—she boasted unceasingly about her famous friendship with the artist Chaim Soutine—nor did she turn up her nose at graffiti artists in her later years. During those long decades of militant modernism, she maintained a happy refuge for those who were nostalgic for Louis Napoleon pompoms and bobbles. And she lived long enough to see her taste vindicated absolutely. ❧

The Divine Madeleine Castaing

MADAME CASTAING'S FANTASY: BARE UPHOLSTERY WADDING NAILED ON THE WALLS, CHAIRS IN NEED OF RECOVERING, FADED DUSTCOVERS, FRAYED CARPETING.

F or many lovers of things modern, a dimly felt decorating urge was apparently awakened while browsing the shelves of certain discount stores (in France, branches of Prisunic), which in 1967 suddenly opened the floodgates to some of the most daring inventions of contemporary design.

These were the first fruits of decorative loopiness. What else could you call the drunken humor of orange and black plastic pedestal footstools, lumpish molded coffee tables, geometric decorative wall panels (orange circles in dark brown squares or vice versa), and those lava lamps with phosphorescent blobs floating around suggestively?

THESE WERE THE FIRST FRUITS OF

This was the era for the jubilant discovery that the smallest detail of everyday life, however mundane, could be thought out, styled, made not only up to date but up to the minute, and could be born again courtesy of vinyl.

In homes given over to this style, guests were obliged to collapse into beanbag chairs or onto rainbow-color cushions piled in the corners. Posters, which like the poor are always with us, became grown-up appurtenances. *Arte povera* indeed, since they really amounted to no more than sheets of paper, posters showed themselves to best advantage among plain white walls and white ceramic-tiled floors so they could jump out at you. Andy Warhol's Pops and Bridget Riley's Ops encouraged a taste for primary colors and simple shapes.

Quintessentially urban, Pop decoration was also an exercise in combinations that were both practical and elegant. Hence the invention of beds that were closets, banquettes that were desks: Everything had to be foldable, recessable, stackable, arrangeable.

DECORATIVE LOOPINESS. ◙

Lucite and brushed steel had their moments of glory. This pre-halogen era was the heyday of the adjustable spotlight whose unforgiving beam was always the starkest of stark white, all the better to highlight gleaming finishes and bright oranges. Huge flowers of mauve and blue were known to embellish bedroom walls, where they matched the fulsome prints on the sheets. The more advanced of the Ops and Pops rediscovered the bent-wood furniture of Thonet (or, more prosaically, bistro furniture) but it was strictly relegated to the kitchen.

This was the period when even Cecil Beaton decided to go modern: He took a shine to tubular furniture and recklessly decided to pair his Aubusson rugs with black velvet walls (he liked his shocking contrasts on the tame side).

It didn't take long for this style to lose its luster as all that plastic started to wear out, and along with it a basic instinct of a society addicted to consumption—the blind confidence in an endless spiral of economic growth as a necessary part of universal progress.

THE SHRIEK OF (SIXTIES) CHIC

Some art historian adept at the old-fashioned but still useful craft of coining scholarly labels on demand will doubtless dub the English designer David Hicks the Master of the Manic Monogram. For indeed, he was one of the first to pursue a policy of INITIALS EVERYWHERE. And since the initials in question were his, he naturally regarded them as a universal sign of good taste. They became a motif worthy of infinite variations and of inclusion in fabrics and other objects with a thoroughness that was nothing short of jubilant.

David Hicks later developed a weakness for herringbone carpets (which today are vaguely evocative of airport waiting rooms), but they fit in well with his systematic use of a single primary color with contrasting white trim for door and window frames. Orange, brighter orange, and chocolate brown were the colors of choice for this very "sixties gentry" style. It was a style of rules. It was deeply concerned with order and delighted in legibility and architectonics: Arches, ribbed vaulting, and keystones were enough to provoke trancelike states in Neo-Palladians who drove Austin Minis with basket-weave sides.

It is to these David Chics that we owe the first profusion of urns, columns, pyramids, and obelisks in all sizes and materials, shapes that inspired everything from waste-baskets to tabletop cigarette lighters (the latter having graduated to nostalgia status nowadays); their very numbers helped ensure that these trophies took a long time to fade from the scene.

Symmetry and order served here as sources of pleasure, and this style was justly famous for its clever ways with storage. Footstools fit under tables, tables collapsed into consoles, that in turn contained secret panels, and on and on.

Tidy, sometimes even fussy, the Chics were delirious with the pleasure of arranging little things in groupings: boxes, cigarette cases, pencil pots, ashtrays, pouches of all kinds, ostrich eggs. And with some pride they would offer to demonstrate nineteen imaginative and tasteful ways to stash their odds and their ends. (Wide-ranging collections of gin bottles were also given this treatment, incidentally, it being considered rather stingy to have only one kind.)

A refined product of a happy time, the style of David Hicks—Oxfordshire squire and lover of garden follies who wears a certain abstemiousness like a badge of opulence—survives today mainly in reruns of British television series from the sixties. It is in these haphazard and satirical versions that it has been handed down to a generation too young to have known the sweetness of living the cult-serial life. ⊞

Tidy, sometimes even fussy, the Chics were delirious with the pleasure of arranging little things in groupings.

The sixties rediscovery of grandfather's high-collared Edwardian shirts paved the way for a renewed appreciation for grandmother's high-styled Edwardian furniture in the next decade.

The early seventies was a time for cleaning out the attic and sprinkling walls and tabletops with the kitsch relics of the turn of the century, especially ones with that melting-before-your-eyes quality so dear to Salvador Dali. Shimmery velvet, old lace, chipped flowery flowerpots, hanging plants, macramé, and quaint old-fashioned embroidery started appearing everywhere.

It was a time for gushing over milk glass, bulbous forms, sinuous motifs, and the floral fantasies of Lalique and Gallé. The blowsy women of Carabin's furniture and the lush overblown products of the school of Nancy provided the perfect decor in which the love generation could have their languorous hallucinations. Those psychedelic posters fit in well with their forebears by Mucha.

Some Neo-Nouveau devotees went for the decadent—the paintings of Gustave Adolphe Mossa and almost anything else that came out of Nice, and the venomous drawings of Alastair, the scrawny turn-of-the-century draftsman of uncertain bloodlines, whom they placed second only to Beardsley. They ate up the eminently tacky stories of Rachilde and her male counterpart, Jean Lorrain, a par-

taker of ether and other embarrassing things.

The Neo-Nouveaus brought the minor decadent and symbolist painters out for one more bow, accumulating reproductions of Knopf and Puvis and following Philippe Jullian's lead in extolling the rehabilitation of Degouve de Nuncques and Lévy-Dhurmer. This may well have been the first generation to serve its design apprenticeship not in museums but in secondhand shops, digging in the archeology of the recent past.

In literature as well, the dreamlike Art Nouveau esthetic lent itself naturally to surrealist interpretations and fit in with the love of the mist-shrouded and the bizarre that were all the rage in those permissive years.

Art Nouveau style was never a great mixer, and it wasn't long before this shortcoming took its toll: As a steady diet, it proved too rich, provoking a certain queasiness the way oversweetened cakes might. Or maybe people found they had swooned just once too often. Before long, Art Nouveau was banished from interiors that pretended to good taste and was shipped off to antiques markets in the provinces, where it swelled the inventories of gleeful secondhand dealers.

The last anachronistic gasp of this discredited craze (call it the last tip of the last sinuous tendril) came in 1994 with the record-breaking Christie's auction of Barbra Streisand's collection. That event, with all its publicity, was doubtless the opening gun of the Neo-Neo-Nouveau style in Iowa, Idaho, and lands beyond. ✳

NEO-NOUVEAU

The early seventies was a time for cleaning out the attic and sprinkling walls and tabletops with the kitsch relics of the turn of the century, especially ones with that melting-before-your-eyes quality so dear to Salvador Dalí.

DISCO DECO

nce again Art Deco took over naturally from Art Nouveau: It was the perfect bracing antidote to all that sinuous sweetness. History repeated itself.

Deco's seventies reprise marked the first time that fashion was the fashion, for homes at least. The Disco Decos dressed their rooms the way they would dress themselves for a night on the town—with the decorating equivalents of wide cuffed pleated pants, platform shoes, fitted jackets, tight shirts and tight sweaters, high waists, long skirts, boleros, bonnets, berets, plucked eyebrows, and bright lipstick. It was contagious, this joyful rediscovery of the era of Dietrich and musical comedies, of the sweet theatricality of coded references, parody and makeup. The smallest one-bedroom apartments were decked out like Busby Berkeley sets. In London, the sixties cult store Biba ran itself into the ground with a repertoire of black and gold even as the bows and fans of this Pseudo-Deco covered everything from matchboxes to telephone receivers.

With the most exacting collectors, Dunand and Ruhlmann abruptly turfed out Majorelle and Gallé. But even the humbler among them went just wild about ebony, macassar, and white satin. They cultivated the nuances of eggshell and off-white and tubular furniture of gleaming chrome. Andy Warhol made this style his own: His actresses, funhouse-mirror reflections of thirties starlets, went through their extravagant paces on the fan-shaped sofas and left behind a little Pan-Cake makeup on the upholstery. And Disco Deco also provided a good reason to reacquaint oneself with the subtleties of French design, with precious materials and fine craftsmanship.

Geometric and vertical, Art Deco certainly never won any prizes for its comfort or for its qualities as a team player: Like Art Nouveau, it didn't tolerate any rivals stealing the spotlight in the name of mixing-and-matching or eclecticism. And so in the end, people got bored with all those thirties bars with potted palms and mirrors and neon signs saying Copacabana and El Morocco. Disco Deco really disappeared when the "disco" part swallowed up the "deco" part.

The first headline-grabbing Art Deco sale ("the property of a couturier-collector") sealed the end of this period. Like the Art Nouveau craze before it, the style today survives only in secondhand shops in towns where they still appreciate thuya-wood furniture carved with fruit reliefs and awkward tables on spindly legs.

THEY CULTIVATED THE NUANCES OF EGGSHELL AND OFF-WHITE AND TUBULAR FURNITURE OF GLEAMING CHROME.

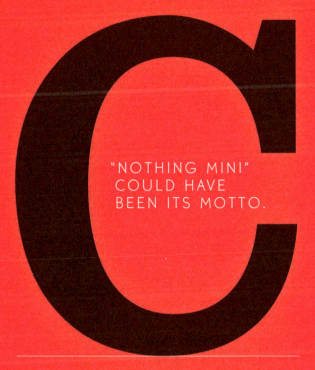

C

"NOTHING MINI"
COULD HAVE
BEEN ITS MOTTO.

onsiderable labor pangs accompanied the birth of a new style, Rothschild-famille, this century's contribution to a pair of famous styles already in existence: "There are two Rothschild styles," wrote the great French chronicler of style Philippe Jullian, "a bright cheerful one, known for *boiserie* and gilt bronze, Savonneries on the floors and Fragonards on the walls, and a more somber version, full of tapestries and huge round-topped chests, Rembrandts and Cellinis." And of course both proclivities have been encouraged assiduously every step of the way by the great antiques dealers like Henri Samuel.

Gone with the Rothschilds

This new style was born at the chance meeting in the Normandy countryside, circa 1970, between an adventuresome young Rothschild wife and an eccentric Englishman with a rolling gait. Ornamental and grandiose, it nonetheless tried to be essentially warm, intimate, and domestic, taking for granted as it did that twelve was the minimum number to qualify as a family group. "Nothing mini," could have been its motto. Brilliantly unconventional mixtures, shameless liberties with proportions, and a free-range eclecticism were its sovereign principles. Which explains how the gold of the wall clocks and chandeliers came to find an unexpected counterpoint in coconut matting. The traditional miles of Genoa velvet and crimson silk were supplanted by prints, prints, prints—a side effect of the era of flower power and its hashish-laden haze. Mint green taffeta curtains played off against harmonies of pinky beige and a virulent red known by the name of Riding Hood. Even the bathrooms, abounding in mahogany and Oriental rugs, seemed to be making up their minds stylistically between Empire and Kathmandu.

Magnifying glasses, walking sticks, orbs of wood and ivory, golf clubs, kitsch figurines—there were so many grouping of objects that even the groupings needed groupings. But that was to be expected in a style that could never bear to skimp on little bronzes or medallions or Biedermeier furniture or Imari porcelain or well-worn leather or ruddy chintz or tufted ottomans or *pietra dura* or big black marble busts or massive consoles by William Kent. Witty trompe l'oeil (objects were painted with dice, playing cards, chess boards, old parchments) took up a theme set forth by the faux-wood finishes on the walls, which were all the more appreciated by being extremely hard to make out.

Geoffrey Bennison, the extremely odd progenitor of this Rothschild hybrid, was not averse to making a personal splash as well. An epicene creature with heavy eyelids and bewigged in carrot orange, he had the look and manners of an oracle-spouting grand-mother (one writer who knew his Greek mythology called him the Teiresias of Pimlico). He received his clients in the back room of his shop in a long robe and high heels. Vicious, but also captivating and endearing, he maintained a court of lost young women of the purest aristo-cratic pedigree and lithe young men with no pedigree at all. So his kingdom was a slightly shadowy no-man's-land between the beau monde and the demimonde. He was a true egalitarian in his way, with a reputation for handing out rough treatment to his clients (all rich of course). There is a story of him shouting at one famously nervous follower, "You're going to have to open up that purse, Dearie."

His sudden demise, in the mid-1980s, cut short the career of this daytime Queen of the Night, this master of delicious decay and why-have-real-when-you-can-concoct-the-faux. His style, called rather cruelly by some "English Madam," was the little-known origin of one of the major themes in interior design today: Shabby Chic. ◆

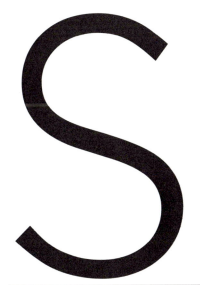

Sir Terence Conran, the dean of multinational decoration, can be compared to those eighteenth-century English trippers of the Grand Tour (a journey whose cultural pretexts did little to disguise its real purpose, which was to flee the fogs of Albion and take advantage of the warmth of the southern countries for as long as possible). The Happy Habitants fall into a distinguished tradition of explorers whom Peter Mayle's book *Toujours Provence* finally provided with a motto and whose approach to the good life definitely includes learning lessons from the natives.

HAPPY HABITAT

A temperate brand of modernism is what seems to suit these English Europhiles, and it is famously in harmony with the simple trappings of the simple life and the fruits of a savoir-faire that dates back to time immemorial. And so old Pernod pitchers, café glasses, glazed earthenware crockery, aluminum coffee pots, painted-wood or garden furniture, rustic sideboards, and armchairs draped in slipcovers work their charms on these lovers of sunny comforts.

Nothing could be further off their mark than little Laura Ashley florals or "genuine" chintz. Functional simplicity, but asceticism-free, is the Happy Habitants' watchword. Nor are these types averse to lofts, loving as they do spaces that are wide open and unencumbered (and easy to maintain). White china dishes, checkered tablecloths, simple hanging light fixtures suit them just fine. They pride themselves on their little wine cellars and happily go off for wine-tasting courses in St.-Rémy-de-Provence or even at Butler's Wharf in London's Docklands.

The kitchen, with its bistro table, is their true living room. Cooking, and taking time and care over it, is their hobby. They are at ease in the present-day world, are against extremes (that is to say both hard-edged modernism and stale traditionalism), and are conscious of their ecological niche: All in all, they bring a degree of extreme refinement to habitat habitation. ◉

> # Functional simplicity, but asceticism-free, is the Happy Habitants' watchword.

The devotee of the loft is an eminently dialectical creature, bound up with modernity, with space and light and pure volumes—the concepts that have formed the basis of modernism since the 1950s—but is also deeply enmeshed with the signs and symbols of the past. Investing as he does in abandoned premises and rehabilitating old rundown neighborhoods, he is really the incarnation of the conservationist spirit.

Artist, photographer, designer, he has found the way to free himself from bourgeois values and from the traditional definitions of what an interior should be in order to invent a new kind of environment and a new way of living in it. Often, the European loft lover is a discreet Americanophile who worships at the altar of those early liberated spirits, the great American painters of the fifties who invented the modern loft by taking disused but affordable warehouses and transforming them into their studios.

Respectful of their surroundings, the lofty ones are generally careful to preserve most of the original distinguishing features: Structural columns and other industrial elements are celebrated by being painted black or white; wood floors are bleached or kept rough; walls are painted white or left in their original brick; and picture windows are allowed to flood the place with bright light. Essentially modern creatures, they have a horror of clutter, knock down every wall and partition, and ruthlessly clear away anything that can stop the line of vision (actually, they typically suffer from a virulent claustrophobia that all these architectural machinations only barely disguise). Their 5,000 square feet usually proves to be beneficial to all concerned, from the imaginative property developer to those fighting to pre-

Lofty

Aspirations

serve historic memory-laden neighborhoods, not to mention the gleeful landlords.

In SoHo, London Docklands, or Montparnasse, this cosmopolitan set find themselves cooking in the living room, making do with a bathroom that is really a bedroom, or having a study that is really a home gym. An upstairs balcony, where one can go to take refuge, is almost a necessary corollary to loft living: In an expanse where the interior feels like an exterior, it is a small nook, shady and protected from all that intimidating light.

As a perfect expression of the 1980s—its size bespeaks wealth and its location bespeaks independence of spirit—the loft today seems to have been tricked by destiny: More and more, it is finding itself crisscrossed with new partitions, nibbled away at by necessary niches, cordoned off and reconfigured until it comes dangerously close to a

> # ESSENTIALLY MODERN CREATURES, THEY HAVE A HORROR OF CLUTTER.

traditional apartment, albeit a spacious one. But loft lovers continue their chic and simple lives without excesses or flourishes even as they adapt their "living spaces" to everyday needs. After an extended bout of the stripped-down esthetic's sober virility, they are discovering with delight some discreetly feminine virtues of the nineties—comfort, warmth, and intimacy.

The 1980s took the role of the perpetual adolescent and played it to the hilt. The Memphisite was like those star students in architecture or design school who delight in tormenting the professor to distraction then prudently back off just before the boom is lowered.

Cultivated, cerebral, quick-witted, and cunning, these designers took a malicious pleasure in making things that defied good sense—conjuring up Otto Wagner, Las Vegas, Buddhist temples, and Sausalito boutiques, slapping Mickey Mouse ears onto skyscrapers, and turning the Empire State Building into a pink plastic dressing table and then pairing it with a white satin bench straight out of a thirties bordello. With mischievous glee they would turn a perfectly tasteful living room into a boxing ring with multicolored columns.

Nothing amused Memphisites more than a teapot inspired by the Glyptothek sculpture garden in Munich or a Dallas dance hall with details from the vaulted ceiling of the Casina of Pius V in the Vatican. No color was allowed that was not shocking, no motif that was not just the least bit dissonant, no sense of scale that was not a little askew. Here was the triumph of the motley collage, the guaranteed surprise on going from outside to inside, the commingling of high and low, colossal and minuscule. Memphis rode a wave of Neo-Just-About-Everything—as if eighteenth-century picturesque had been revived in a dream by a petro-sheik from the Emirates and adapted for the tastes of Hong Kong.

But Memphis also paved the way for the triumphal if sometimes deconstructed return of ornament, a naughty indifference to the rules, the piling on of detail, and the hoarding of styles in bits and pieces. Everything became a means of taking orthodoxies of all persuasions and cutting them to shreds. It was almost impossible in those years to find a builder's model apartment without a room of blank walls in pure colors reminiscent of a meditation chamber in Rajasthan, a futuristic bathroom worthy of Houston, a Felix the Cat nursery, or a deconstructed living room with a ziggurat vase enthroned on a wobbly table whose legs were modeled after the insects in fifties science-fiction movies, while on the stove a cleverly phallic gas lighter stood ready to shoot sparks under the tea kettle.

The Memphis kick, playful as it was, ended up by gracing suburban kitchens with a few touches of Tyrian pink and bright turquoise. And like Art Deco before it and forties powder-puff-Louis after it, the Memphis style went for its final close-up at Sotheby's in Monte Carlo, at Karl Lagerfeld's great divestiture of 1991. ❧

> ## Cultivated, cerebral, quick-witted, and cunning, these designers took a malicious pleasure in making things that defied good sense.

Just as surely as there is a Perpendicular Gothic, there exists an Ovoid Futuristic. It is known by its extremism and its tapered egglike shapes—childish science-fiction fantasy meets a fetish for technology: Picture an aerodynamic production of *Oedipus* designed by Philippe Starck, and you won't be far wrong.

Speeds unknown to man, realms unheard of, and the otherwise novel are its only values. Whereas most decorators are by nature attracted to any object or piece of furniture with the slightest pedigree or any association with the past that they can leech on to, these fierce futurists see anything that wasn't born tomorrow as phobia material and the stuff of mawkish sentimentality. There is nothing they hate more than a Tang horse on a Louis XVI chest, which to them are no different from a glass figurine resting on a lace doily in the concierge's room at the bottom of the stairs.

The Starshipper has a pronounced predilection for merciless expanses, gleaming surfaces of polished marble, shining metal or epoxy, empty walls with vases in the shape of bomb casings bolted onto them. The more blank and uncommunicative the material, the more he likes it. If the space in question is a public one, like a hotel or museum, he dreams of staffing it full of aeronautical engineers (with great-looking hats and flight suits, of course) who can patrol like the housekeeping staff armed with bottles of Windex to hunt down the smallest fingerprint.

He dreams a world in which nothing shows, especially no flaw, and in which four spotless walls (maybe placed at a slight angle) encapsulate all that is necessary for life. Compactness stands for absolute truth.

For the Starshipper, the world is never quite logical enough: Everything should be meaningful and efficient and as smooth as a marble tombstone. So it is an ideal destined always to meet with disappointment. Like an eighteenth-century philosopher fascinated by the incommensurability of the universe, he asks nothing more than to be able to rest on a tailwing stool and contemplate the awesomeness of a smooth and shining basalt monolith. His is an architecture of human insignificance, and it proclaims that man is nothing but a fingerprint on the surface of things—a fingerprint that a malevolent deity, armed with Windex, can wipe out with a simple flick of a dustcloth.

THESE FIERCE FUTURISTS SEE ANYTHING THAT WASN'T BORN TOMORROW AS PHOBIA MATERIAL AND THE STUFF OF MAWKISH SENTIMENTALITY.

Starship NASA

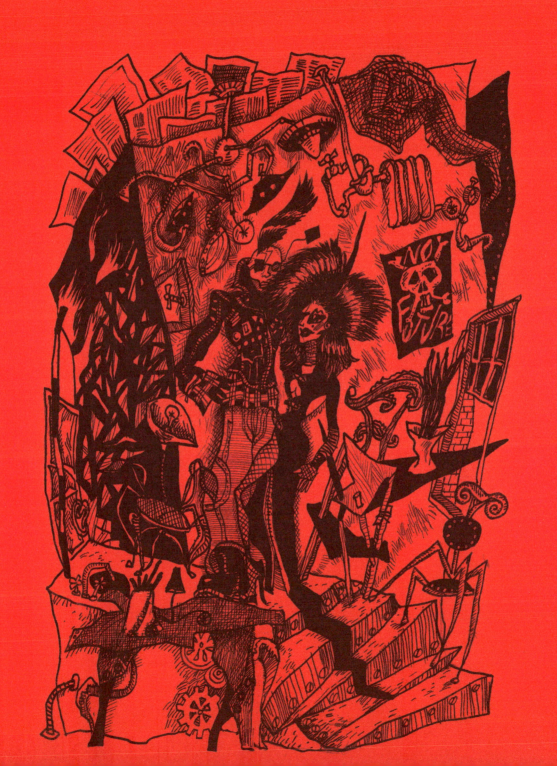

England is known as a country with a genius for making the most out of almost anything. It is also a place with a strong belief in free expression and manual work: Things that in France would be relegated to little pottery or macramé workshops in a few small towns high in the Lubéron cross the Channel to receive a retrospective exhibition at the V & A and lend their name to an important new school of esthetics.

How else would you explain the incredible liberties of personal appearance taken daily on the streets of London, which are populated by ghouls with spiked hair, specters dressed up like undertakers, the distracted-looking bat-blind, and assorted loonies decked out in riots of color that put parrots to shame. In a country like that, where nothing old is ever discarded and nothing new ever created, the only avenue for experimentation or consolation is to celebrate the dregs and to fashion treasures out of trash.

Tilted windows, zigzag tables, shattered countertops— they all screamed, "Haywire Rules!"

It is this need for self-expression (or maybe it's more like self-expressionism) that inspires those paint-splattered apartments whose walls are inlaid with aluminum foil and newspaper clippings, Tibetan mandalas, and other ethnic gleanings, where nothing can withstand the gravitational pull of collage, the pleasure of juxtaposition, the rage for layering. If not exactly chaos theory, it is certainly patchwork theory in action.

The same influences were felt in high-flown London design circles, circa 1988, which worshipped destructionism the way Dante worshipped his Beatrice. Who could forget those jewelry stores where the sparkles of gems matched the glint of the broken glass that was artfully scattered here and there and whose sharp edges were more scary than any alarm system? Tilted windows, zigzag tables, shattered countertops—they all screamed, "Haywire Rules!"

One found the same thing in Covent Garden art studios that combined the winsomeness of troglodyte garages with the charm of fallout shelters: Scraps of rusted metal, wire, unfinished assemblages, and half-fused sculp- WORLD'S END tures were everywhere in those places. If it could grate, grind, or clank, it was welcome. Less memorable were the pedestal tables inspired by the less-than-universal appeal of comic-book monsters or those crude, uncomfortable stools. Is this what they meant by the old motto "Let your dreams soar up to the stars"?

The World's End esthetic brings to mind those stories that are always showing up in the newspaper, where pieces of conceptual art are mistaken for trash by the janitor and carefully carted away. It was always hard to imagine the future of these interiors whose only comfort derives from the sense of quiet resignation embodied in their motto: "No future."

Minimalism was to decoration what Zen is to philosophy. Searing and definitive, trafficking in ultimates and crackling with electricity, it presented itself as the moral side of esthetics. And so it functioned as the last refuge for those whose spirits were uneasy and saturated with things, for those who responded to the constant assaults of consumerism by rising above it all and celebrating scarcity.

There were some decorators and arbiters of style (unconscious swingers, of the Hegelian pendulum variety) who affirmed that everything had already been done and said and that they had found decor's Absolute Truth: In other words, they had seen the end of history and it was floored in tatami. Their interiors strove for a mute eloquence, for the silence that is worth a thousand words, and looked for it with a sense of restriction equivalent in its way to the limitations placed on thought in old-fashioned Jesuit boarding schools. A few discreet frames signaling doors, cupboards, and windows; movable partitions; a lightbulb here, a hint of a sleeping alcove there; a hollowed-out stone for a bath (appointed with scream-for-mercy brushes); the trademark wooden bucket.

MINIMALISM TO THE MAX

IT FUNCTIONED AS THE LAST REFUGE FOR THOSE WHOSE SPIRITS WERE UNEASY AND SATURATED WITH THINGS.

This cult of pure line and space barred even the shadow of a shameful ornament or unnecessary object from its realm of stoic silence. Its devotees sought redemption in futons, meditation in cooking, metaphysical enlightenment in cleanliness. (A style like this would never have caught on were it not for the *liaison dangereuse* between it and Anglo-Saxon Puritanism, which contributed even more ways to impose strictures.)

It is hard to dissociate the minimalist vogue from the taste for Japanese design that swept the world in about 1980 with about the same anemic allure as a terminal illness: the reduction of color into shades of black and charcoal gray (if possible washed out with water filtered through volcanic rock), the abandonment of line in favor of shapelessness, brutal (and voracious) deconstructionism. They all provided pretexts for still more purification rituals.

The only thing one can add about this movement of voluntary catatonia, whose attraction remains a mystery to this day, is that many of those interiors ended up being transformed, somewhere around the middle of 1991, into a cross between the stage sets of Bébé Bérard and the salon of Madame de Pompadour. ❳❲

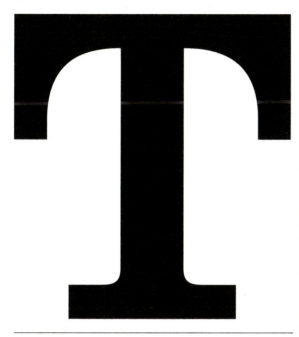

Anything subtle or "historical" (translation: pre-1945) makes them dizzy.

The lovers of this style delight in viewing the world in the colors of their favorite comic strip. Just as the Gluckists and Piccinists once forced the choice between French opera and Italian, the Jukeboxers have a way of dividing humanity into two groups—Tintinists and Dick Tracyists—followers, they argue, of two totally irreconcilable world views.

In general, the Jukeboxers are young or think of themselves as young, and they firmly shut the door to the world of ideas. Anything termed intellectual is anathema. Anything subtle or "historical" JUKEBOX (translation: pre-1945) makes them dizzy. They live in a state of perpetual adolescence designed by Raymond Loewy: a Studebaker on steroids, a chrome orange squeezer with meat-grinder looks, a late-Stalinist toaster—these all send them into ecstasies. To please them, something must be Formica, linoleum, loud plastic, shiny aluminum, or a futurist form from forty years ago.

They have programmed into their brains a little shelf of paperbacks—rebellious adventures by J. D. Salinger or tough-guy crime novels by Boris Vian—and they have developed the power to astonish with their encyclopedic knowledge of cult TV serials of the sixties, which for them are talismans of culture. While they are always searching for new mythologies, the ones they find always come either from America or the movies. Their loves are pretty much confined to the animated (in both senses of the word), the energetic, the pulsating—the more hopped-up the better. They shy away from such a thing as discourse, and will explain with an unaccustomed gravity that they "think visually," a catchphrase that barely masks a contempt for articulate forms of expression.

Immune to the charms of rhetoric, they are nonetheless unconscious masters of the decorative oxymoron—the shined-up motorbike in the living room or a Wurlitzer jukebox in a yellow-tiled bathroom. ☉

I n 1936, Charles de Beistegui, that capricious French multimillionaire and party giver to whose tastes one and all deferred, commissioned Le Corbusier to design him an apartment that incorporated a complete set of Baroque trappings, including girandoles and Bohemian crystal, Venetian furniture and Second Empire poufs—everything, down to the octagonal walls, that could not be more repellent to that poet of the right angle.

The result, a bizarre contradiction in terms with Champs-Élysées views, is famous to this day. It also marked the first wave of the rejection of the modern, a reaction that swept to victory half a century later thanks to people of style who knew the difference between the esthetic and the ascetic. For by that time, standard-issue modernism had become a catch-all label for every kind of mediocrity, and the excuse for lack of imagination and poverty of vocabulary, while its promoters used the sacred myth of economy of means as a convenient excuse for its shortcomings. Designs that started out bland and were then subjected to majority rule (that is to say, the lowest, emptiest common denominator) simply started to wear thin.

And so the world saw a triumphal return of ornament, which encompassed every trick in the book from the Greek to Alfred Jarry's hallucinatory pataphysics with a jubilation bordering on the perverse. Grainy metal, shiny black paint, and the tonalities of extinct volcanoes suddenly found themselves shoved aside by painted plaster, gilt bronze, random reliefs of heads and cabochons—a lexicon of fantasy adapted directly from the discreet ornamentalists of the fifties. The second death of Adolf *(Ornament and Crime)* Loos paved the way for the second coming of Louis XVII, the Grecian-drag of Emilio Terry furniture, and set-design theatricality gone wild. Fun conquered Grimness over the Ruins of Modern Good Taste.

This victory unleashed a magical (or perhaps totemic) artistic torrent that incorporated ancient esoteric symbols, moons, stars, a bit of neo-Etruscan here and there, and whose lack of comfort almost equaled that of the Bauhaus. Everyone had to bring forth his own mythical vocabulary—but because these Borromini-come-latelies had never mastered the art and craft of allusion in the way postwar artists had, Neo-Baroque has always teetered on the edge of Rococo Rock, if not Neo–Candy Box. ✳

> EVERYONE HAD TO BRING FORTH HIS OWN MYTHICAL VOCABULARY.

**"I** am a clapped-out Eros." So said Hamlet, or at least the symbolist Hamlet as presented in the writings of Jules Laforgue. And that could be the motto of this distinctly British approach to decorating, in which the threadbare and the faded have advanced beyond preference to the point of fetish.

Its virtues are vaunted and flaunted with an admirable constancy by that mischievous British organ of contemporary taste *The World of Interiors*. With great fierceness, it proclaims the end of decorating schemes plotted out on graph paper, of formulas of all kinds, of stylistic rules and regulations, of hackneyed symmetries, matchings, coordinates, and all decorative effects that shout like billboards—in other words, it is the natural enemy of petit-bourgeois tidiness, of keeping up appearances and costs.

SHABBY CHIC

This is a style that scorns the clean and the carefully dusted in favor of rooms that are used every day and improve with age, objects that are broken down and patched up and possessed of a little Socratic grime, places that show the tracks of time and emotions. This is decor for those who were "born too late" and who are fixated on the images and sensations of childhood, who love the kinds of old places that by their very nature douse the fires of renovating zeal and property speculation. It's a view that is militant, stubborn, even ecological (call it the decor equivalent of composting). The worn-out kilim, the lumpy sunken sofa, the water

> ## This is decor for those who were "born too late."

stains on the ceiling, the faded fabric, the genially patched and peeling paint, the poetically chipped china—they all proclaim a determined and almost political predilection for love among the ruins.

Though generally conservation-minded and enlightened, Shabby Chic doesn't always escape today's foolish obsession with authenticity and pedigree. But by combining in its ranks the leathery old spinster, the esthete whose mandarin ways stop just short of foot-long Manchu fingernails, the slightly overwhelmed lord of the manor, and stray romantics of all stripes, Shabby Chic is certainly in the vanguard of ecumenism if nothing else. 🦅

**F**or many decades the masters of decoration were the French. From the end of the war until the end of the sixties, the House of Jansen reigned supreme, and the names Geffroy, Boudin, and Delbée were all one needed as a guarantee of highest quality. And indeed it was these men that the Englishman John Fowler used to cite in his early days, when he felt called upon, despite his horsy jaw and exquisite manners, to invoke an authoritative precedent.

A man of humble origins, John Fowler made himself indispensable to society women, first by his unique mastery of the art and science of off-white so dearly loved by clients of Syrie Maugham and also, of course, by the excellence of his taste. Nevertheless, it took two formidable women, Sybil Colefax (Lady Colefax, actually) and Nancy Lancaster, to fix his rendezvous with decorative destiny.

Nancy Lancaster was born in Virginia and spent some of her schooldays in France, settling in England in the mid-1920s. After accumulating husbands and houses, she decided she preferred the latter, they being after all more durable. A Southerner through and through, it was her custom to raise the Confederate flag each morning. And it was to those exotic origins that she attributed her taste for comfort and for well-used things. She exposed her sofas and settees to the rain and the open air, put slipcovers and cushions in the sun to fade, steeped her chintz in tea—anything to make something seem worn out. The design world is still feeling the effects of that delicious paradox that made an American from the South the muse (and owner) of the London design firm of Colefax & Fowler, the fountainhead of that quintessentially British style, Shabby Chic.

Fowler, with whom she formed what her aunt Nannie (Lady Astor) called the most mismatched couple she had ever seen who weren't married, balanced her radical tendencies with his own passion—perhaps of Freudian origin, who knows?—for Marie Antoinette, both person and style. He used to explain how the "masculinity" of English furniture found its "feminine" counterpart in French taste. He adored, for example, the color taupe (Nancy Lancaster

"Be Still, My Chintz" | AT ITS BEST, NOTHING IS MORE FRAGILE THAN THE COLEFAX & FOWLER BLEND OF ENGLISH COUNTRY HOUSE AND CLASSIC HIGH FRENCH TASTE SOFTENED BY THE SHADES OF ITALY. | ⚜

referred to it as "elephant's breath," and dubbed some of his other favorite shades "dauphin's caca" and "queen's vomit"). A crossbreeding of these two fierce bloodlines could not fail to produce a style with universal drawing power.

And it was to the keeping of this double flame that Fowler's heirs have devoted themselves with the seriousness of cardinals in conclave. No fabric, wallpaper, furniture, or object in their interiors must be allowed to escape the "total look" of Colefax & Fowler. Nothing new is added into the canon that has not been meticulously weighed, measured, and dissected and its origin traced with a philological rigor to an eighteenth-century paint fragment found in the hinterlands of Portugal or to a stray antique domino that came to light by accident in the renovation of the former washhouse of some early-nineteenth-century manor. This rather severe method nonetheless results in Kent vicarages filled with chintz with large roses and duchesses' boudoirs covered in twig-patterned wallpaper.

At its best, nothing is more fragile than the Colefax & Fowler blend of English country house and classic high French taste softened by the shades of Italy. It has been kept going by a commendable attention to detail and history and nurtured every step of the way by a fearsome public relations effort. Fowler himself, who always seemed to be going from financial ruin to financial ruin, would be more surprised than anyone at the current bankability of a quintessentially British style and company that are precision-engineered with a rigor that is actually totally German.

ertified classics are the only objects that gain admittance to these intense and high-strung rooms that are usually the creations of a carefully stylized decoratrix clad in skyscraper heels and a little black dress (with dark glasses to match on days when she is especially tired, which is to say every day).

These are women who are always vaguely mysterious but always terribly modern in every way. Their fear about keeping up appearances (in every sense of the word) has bound them in the service of some extremely jealous gods. So being in a constant state of anxiety, they have come to revere certain icons: Le Corbusier chaises longues, Eileen Gray rugs, Reitveld chairs, and any piece of furniture by Chareau as long as it has lots of tubes. The miracles attributed to these relics were first recorded half a century ago and have never been surpassed in the world of the modern—that is to say, the only world that counts. (And these masters, terribly misunderstood in their own day, owe their resurgence to the devotion of these austere prophetesses.) All this is not to say that the Sure-Fires lack a sense of humor—but the smile is out of the corner of the mouth and the twinkle is in the corner of the eye. No giggling lapse is permitted to weaken their seriousness of purpose.

Being bilingual and bicontinental, they are resigned to a permanent state of jet lag as one of the inevitable stigmata of their success. And not ones for taking risks, they limit their palette to a range that can't miss: gray, beige, gray-beige, white, and the mother of all colors—black. Marked as they are by intelligence and flawless timing, they have learned how to prosper in an economy of means. But one also knows, somehow, that somewhere in their past they have known moments of intoxicating ecstasy.

SURE-FIRE CHIC

They limit their palette to a range that can't miss: gray, beige, gray-beige, white, and the mother of all colors—black.

C

ease-Fire Chic is the return to normalcy that follows Sure-Fire's shock tactics. Here, Harmony and Taste compete for Man's favors.

Essentially a conformist, the Cease-Fire devotee holds simple lines, pure volumes, and natural materials as articles of faith. Eminently civilized and versed in history, he pays never-ending homage to Jean-Michel Frank (whose ideas his things loot shamelessly), to primitivism as long as it is in good taste, and to rarefied pieces of Art Deco (which he prefers to call Cubist). The width of his horizons is bound by his admiration for certain of the great masters: Matisse, Picasso, and Braque. He's always ready with raptures about the blue of Matisse's *Femmes d'Alger* (which he describes as "indescribable") and venerates a scrap of a paper tablecloth that

CEASE-FIRE CHIC

A moderate man,

has been authentically dated from the period of *Demoiselles d'Avignon*.

without its excesses.

he practices modernism

A moderate man, he practices modernism without its excesses. Yes, he has things in leather and corroded metal, but his heart really belongs to the warmer charms of exotic woods, of which his pieces incorporate every known variety.

In these interiors, an African mask (an idea straight from the thirties) offers a welcome bit of visual punch. Bare walls with one or two plaster casts, a pair of foliate plaster lamps, upholstery of flannel and sheepskin, beiges, natural tones, a flash of iridescent something or other—each adds its particular richness to this measured and urbane universe. In France (and elsewhere among those who long for the French lessons of yesteryear), a Gallimard volume or two—creamy beige covers wrapping uncut pages—blends in perfectly. Certain decorating magazines are kept on hand ready to testify to the rightness of all he surveys.

Exhausted by the months of hard work and by the constant inexplicable need to reassure self and others of his originality, he makes regular restorative getaways to Tangier or Marrakech (shades of Matisse again!) where he gorges himself on minor orientalists and fierce charcoal drawings by Paul Jouve. ≋

nineteenth-century American rural idyll and the eighteenth-century Swedish royal court are not one and the same thing.

This statement, somewhat obvious on the face of it, nonetheless must have come as a surprise to the average reader of *Elle* and *Marie-Claire*, which chose to reveal two newly discovered brands of exoticism—Shaker and Gustavian—at the same moment.

Both of these styles sprang into view during the years when decorative nature worship was fashionable and one was expected to celebrate light woods and rough, not to say crude, materials. And it is true that both styles are eminently sensible, reserved, spare, and agreeable—in short, just what the doctor ordered for a society suddenly plunged into crisis, whose center was everywhere and whose boundaries were nowhere.

Shaker is a total esthetic, well thought out and meditated upon, tempered and temperate. Everything the average home of today needs—spinning wheels, wooden brooms, farm tools—were suddenly transformed into works of art by the Good Fairy of Utility, who works only in cherrywood or pear. The Shakers had design before there was design, rekindling the possibilities of blond wood and magically joining it to forms that are at once thoroughly modern and exquisitely nostalgic as symbols of a rural utopia that knew how to keep its desires under control.

The Shakers' main indulgences seem to have been knobs, from which, with great abandon, they hung their chairs and brooms. Their huge but perfectly proportioned chests with the little round pulls, their baskets and oval boxes in many sizes, these all remain emblems of a universe in which everything was calm and scrubbed and people contented themselves with the essentials. The world of the Shakers therefore had all the ingredients of a perfect myth for our society of excess.

The Shaker style was an avatar—and a very graceful one at that—of the contamination-phobic concern with hygiene, the latent Puritanism, and creeping guilt that are so much a part of domestic life today. When one thinks of it that way, it is no surprise how the Shakers got their name: They had a great deal to shake about.

Everything the average home of today needs— spinning wheels, wooden brooms, farm tools—were suddenly transformed into works of art. ≣

"

’s all been seen, it’s all been done, it’s all been flogged to death. With all the exotic looks that had been rediscovered, overestimated and revived by the end of the eighties, there wasn’t that much left for those who live and breathe the latest style revelation. So the public was all too ready to seize on and wax ecstatic over something that can only be an oxymoron: the exotic North.

That is the only possible explanation for the way this Swedish offshoot of Louis XVI style was bizarrely catapulted into a major design trend. For despite all its soberness, this frigid esthetic found itself transformed into the "young style" par excellence, equally suitable for the young aristocrat who was sick of all those tired rosewood desks and boulle-boulle-boulle from the family château and for the high-strung single career woman who imbued this white-painted furniture with a newfound dignity.

Star of the North

Take some freshly scrubbed and bleached floorboards, curtains of cotton or linen in farmer’s-daughter gingham, furniture unencumbered by subtleties, some lightweight prints, soft pastels, a few etchings, white pottery, and simple flawless glassware—and before you knew it you had a genuine look that was neat, tidy, soothing, practical, inexpensive, and domestic to the core. It was remarkable for its lack of pretensions, a quality much appreciated among fashion folk (for whom simplicity is the ultimate affectation).

A style that would ordinarily have been no more than a footnote to the history of decoration instead launched a thousand white boutiques specializing in cream-colored dishes and tiles, to say nothing of the hyperborean hypermarkets that have made a specialty of this genre. Everything that could be (and some things that could not) was stripped, brushed, scoured, and painted without mercy.

No one would have been more surprised than the Star of the North himself, Gustav III, to see how his taste was fueling this esthetic of "unbearable lightness" and austerely cute welfare-state hygienics. But in fact it arrived on the scene just in time: In a culture where everything from detergents to milk to makeup remover has to be organic—why not interiors as well?

EVERYTHING THAT COULD BE (AND SOME THINGS THAT COULD NOT) WAS STRIPPED BRUSHED, SCOURED, AND PAINTED WITH OUT MERCY. *

In the 1980s, it wasn't enough to be rich: One wanted to be cosmopolitan as well. Design needed to exude both qualities in order to satisfy the escapist whims of hordes of freshly minted yuppies (young urban professionals) who were as yet unaware that, thanks to the coming recession, they were about to become puppies (poor urban professionals).

These monolingual citizens of the world discovered the charms of what the French call *travèlerailleting* (in German: *trawelreiting*), a quintessentially middlebrow Anglo-Saxon genre that provided a somewhat dignified outlet for their silly (though thankfully limited) impulse to roam. They found it far simpler to let the young Evelyn Waugh do their globe-trotting for them, which is why the output of this born-again stay-at-home found a new lease on life: His acrid colonial tales and accounts of Abyssinian rumblings came out in new editions one after the other, along with Robert Byron's Sumerian roamings and the nostalgic waxings of any Colonel Blimp with memories of Borneo in the Fabulous Fifties. And so it was that Bruce Chatwin was elevated to the international pantheon of literature.

This was the time to be in the hotel business—or at least in the hotel *renovation* business: Everywhere, hostelries chic and not-so-chic were spiffed up in the hope. that some of those armchair thrill-seekers might actually leave home for a night or two. And from these establishments a recognizably eighties style emerged: a deft hybrid of average Italian spa town, wooded Frankfurt suburb and Texas desperado, with a dab of English country house as seen on TV serials.

Muzak style saw the triumph of mahogany-veneer Regency, dumbed-down colonial, great tubs of artificial flowers, surfaces lacquered in eggplant and light almond green, wall-to-wall carpeting as far as the eye could see, faux-authentic brass mounts by the gross. Any piece of furniture that could be upholstered became incurably afflicted with "fresh" prints or loud chintz.

This pathological need for freshness everywhere was most expensively evident in the proliferation of garden rooms, with their tedious catalogues of latticework on the walls and windows. With all those glass roofs, the watchword of the era could well have been "The Greenhouse Effect Begins at Home." The chief crop of this bell-jar gardening was admirable, eloquent, and totally synthetic plastic variegated bamboo. And what a memorable meeting of opposites it was—green yet white, simple yet sophisticated, primitive yet available by the yard in strips.

Painted wood and metal; fake stained glass; rooms planned to match the designs on plastic placemats; the glare of American-style spotlights that, though pointed at the cream-colored ceilings, derived their only sense of pity from rheostats; servants from countries unheard of by their employers; torrents of pneumonia-promoting air-conditioning; room scents courtesy (or discourtesy) of Crabtree & Evelyn; the lancinating but inescapable murmur of Muzak—all these were finishing touches on the decor lingua franca of the age. ✿

MUZAK
A deft hybrid of average Italian spa town, wooded Frankfurt suburb and Texas desperado, with a dab of English country house as seen on TV serials.

KING OF THE MODE

What is fashion, after all, if not an *affaire de décor*?

Since the day eighty years ago when Jacques Doucet had his Damascus Road–like conversion from Fragonard to Picasso, through Jeanne Lanvin's butterfly-studded dressing table, to Chanel and Schiaparelli and beyond—the annals of style have bulged with virtuosos of couture whose homes have been the talk of the town. Fabulous reports of these interiors have been systematically magnified and mythologized by media voracious for anything photogenic to trumpet, by a public hungry for anything new to spend money on, and by the ever-growing fashion for fashion—until there is no way to escape the ascendancy of a new aristocracy, the lords of the rag trade. Its members are a fabulous crowd, carrying in their wake a bevy of top models and what used to be called the beautiful people. They have risen like cream to the top of a society that reveres the insignificant, and in scale at least they can only be compared to ancient potentates who, like them, had the means to indulge their grandiose caprices.

The homes of the couture kings have one essential in common: Like the daughter of Zeus, they suddenly spring up fully formed (that is to say, fully photographed) down to the last toaster and baldachined Porthault-sheeted bed. They obey one rule only, the rule of The Most: Everything must be The Most unusual, The Most hard to procure, The Most fabulous example of its kind, The Most expensive. No object is allowed that does not stand out and has not been destined since its creation to pulverize a record at some future auction—proof, as if proof were needed in these circles, that superior taste and an eagle eye were a legitimate value added tax.

Within these heady guidelines, the couture interior is actually quite eclectic, though always rarefied and showing the way to as-yet-unheard-of trends. In a manner that is dignified and controlled, it takes in its stride a canvas by Goya (the last one in private hands, of course), a Royère armchair from the fifties, Matisse collages and Renaissance bronzes, chairs by Carlo Bugatti and drawings by Ingres, straw marquetry and Gobelins tapestries.

If the law of the exceptional is abandoned for anything, it is only for the law of extremes—to create a Louis XVI palace on a desert island, a log dacha in the Canaries, or a palapa hut in Iceland. Neither the expense nor the effort is even noticed, so total is their power, so deep their pockets.

But in the end, couture interiors prove to be all too mortal: They sink without a trace as quickly as they have risen, the sets are struck as easily as they are mounted. For they are after all just dream sequences of the kind you see knitted out of vapors on the stage, casualties of the built-in sense of boredom and cricket-length attention spans that are the wages of daily contact with the world of fashion. These houses are in a way not really houses at all, but more like allegories or morality tales: Their lesson is how much more things possess us than we possess them, how in truth we only rent that which we own, that the world is really just a waiting room, and that this lifetime is really just a turn on the runway.

THE RULE OF THE MOST: EVERYTHING MUST BE THE MOST UNUSUAL, THE MOST HARD TO PROCURE, THE MOST FABULOUS EXAMPLE OF ITS KIND, THE MOST EXPENSIVE.

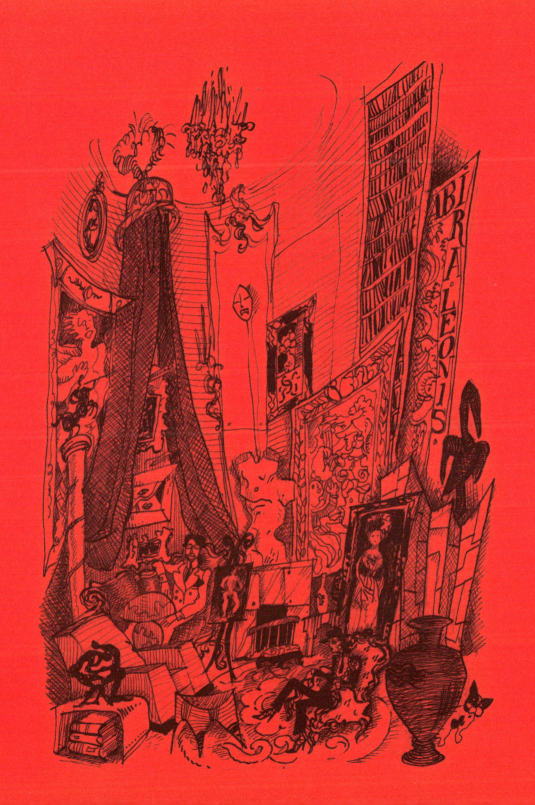

Embarrassing as it might be to both parties, there are similarities between the Philadelphians and the couture kings.

The Philadelphians, however, are endowed with a certain decorous sense of shame. How hard it is for them to allow a brazen—that is to say, visible—display of the dirty laundry of their wealth. If they were New Englanders, they would line up for a scarlet letter, and that letter would be *W*. And were they not so burdened with their distinguished European lineages, they would probably just go wild with indulgence and furnish their houses like the Shakers. But as it is, Philadelphia families have Thomas Jefferson's neoclassical example to take comfort in.

Their floors are dark and highly waxed, their walls plain and off-white. They consider it proper to hang sets of architectural drawings as long as the buildings in question aren't ones they built themselves. Academic nudes cheer up the more private spaces, like the library and the bathrooms—sensuality is fine as long as it has a college education. The furniture is of mahogany, neoclassical or Louis XVI. Urns of all types (not excluding Egyptian canopic jars) in marble or rare wood are set off by bits of Georgiana (mostly knife boxes and tea caddies), while a collection of swords adds a decorative but manly touch. And there are numerous busts and statues in plaster, a material highly prized for its lack of color and appreciated for the way its ivory tones shimmer and ripple through the classical lexicon.

In houses like these, caught in the shadow of holy understatement, it's the Greek torsos scattered in the garden that seem to be having the most fun.

PHILADELPHIA STORY

Sensuality is fine as long as it has a college education.

The Empire style is still flourishing, with the help of a few steroids and a troop of bachelors who reside in grand apartments off the western edges of the boulevard St.-Germain. This is a crowd nostalgic for the golden age of Frenchiosity, fanatic about good diction and proper style, and voracious in their consumption of tomes of history and memoirs that preserve for their wallowing pleasure the burnished echoes of past glories and of a late-lamented *savoir-vivre*.

This is a style that is manly to the extreme—and, indeed, sometimes a little too buffed to be believed. With its heavy lines and slathered-on gilding, it has taken on a pedigree of its own.

That famous bird of ill omen Mario Praz (whose appearance in a park could cause helicopters to tumble from the sky and whose entrance into a room caused the pieces to fall from the chandeliers) was the first critic and scholar to deem the Empire style in urgent need of revival. Professor Praz, who in his books became the caustic and funereal resuscitator of the long-forgotten charms of Murat (erstwhile king of Naples) and Empress Marie Louise, would no doubt be shocked and delighted to see how his elegies for these and other Napoleonic near-greats would inspire one of the grand style hyperboles of the 1980s, a period rife with hyperboles (and of nouveaux riches to indulge them).

The opulence of the rich Milanese, usually kept well hidden behind heavy gray forbidding walls, suddenly blossomed into New Look Empire—all breccian marble, gleaming gilt, Pompeiian atriums, and Canova-style Ledas. Never short of historical references

NAPOLEON IS ALIVE AND WELL AND SUMMERING ON LAKE COMO

(which are all the more numerous for being so superficial), New Look Empire also finds room under its swanlike wing for objects of Grand Tour and Egyptian Campaign kitsch—obelisks and pyramids, dancing fauns, and flexing gladiators. And how well they look against a background of sponge paintings of stylized ruins or scenes of lewdity inspired by the Villa dei Misteri.

The favorite settings for these image-laden extravaganzas are colonnaded courtyarded villas on the Italian lakes. Their interiors are dripping with paintings by obscure students of David, heroic bronzes and fragments of ancient statues, grimacing Minervas and fearsome gorgons, gleaming shields and round reliefs of lions' heads, Grecian daybeds and porphyry libation bowls that look fresh from the offices of the imperial architects Percier & Fontaine. Think Visconti's saturation-decoration going Greek or of the sainted memory of the archeologist J. J. Winckelmann, the first of the classical esthetes to pay with his life for his love of beauty. In clever enough hands and punched up with bright colors, this ornamental bag of tricks sometimes earns its keep as well: At least one designer-householder was able to make it the basis of a highly profitable line of plates and dish towels.

Lake Como Empire has extended the influence of France to the four corners of the overdecorated world. Its resonance is felt even in America, where it is described as "so Las Vegas it belongs in Miami." ♛

A period rife with hyperboles (and of nouveaux riches to indulge them).

A nother of those crash-landing styles, and one of the messier ones at that.

The Junk Junkies are decoration addicts who know every nuance, adore every fad, revere every style before getting bored and moving on to the next, and believe in satiating every one of the senses with-out restraint. They have read every book on the

The Junk Junkies

decorative arts and also, alas, every shelter magazine. And they delight in rarefication upon rar-efication: Chintz must be ancient, taffetas must be pigeon-throat gray or squashed-flea-sigh umber, velvets of preference are those exhumed from old basement vaults.

They try to be casual but always end up giving in to their compulsions, not without a certain bitter ruefulness. You can see them before sunrise at the Bermondsey Market in London with spelunkers' lamps and pockets full of magnifying glasses, or pacing like caged pumas around the edges of small town antiques fairs several hours before opening time.

Like all creatures who live on raw instinct, they are ruthless toward their fellow stalkers and are endowed with keen senses of smell, hearing, and vision. They have only one phobia—

NOTHING INTERESTS THEM THAT IS NOT DECREPIT, RICKETY, SCRATCHED, IF NOT DOWNRIGHT DUBIOUS.

anything that is stamped or signed with the name of a reputable source. Nothing interests them that is not decrepit, rickety, scratched, if not downright dubious. Original paint on anything is a bonus, an original box, the jackpot. While many people would be embarrassed to be found buying their furnishings in the faubourg St.-Antoine or on the Lower East Side, these people have a loathing of the faubourg St.-Honoré and Madison Avenue. They don't mind admitting they are antistyle and helpless in the face of a must-have object. "It's too much for me" is their plaintive cry as they go down in flames while reaching for their wallets.

Among their pronounced weaknesses are Victorian papier-mâché, painted wood, old gilt, trinkets made of shells, kitsch Egyptomania (especially anything that looks mummified), old Christmas ornaments, saucy figurines, and picture calendars from 1935.

Infinite juxtaposition is their art form: They're the ones who can put an Edwardian boarding house soup tureen together with a Byzantine monstrance and make it look the ultimate in chic. Desperadoes like these are more to be pitied than censured. ✣

There exists, in France at least, a generation whose every retrograde sensory nerve can be set atingling by the mere mention of two redolent words, "Sanyas" and "Popot."

This double-barreled name belonged to a now-defunct Paris furniture shop whose exuberant advertisements used to jump out of the pages of that sometimes-bombastic organ of fifties good taste *Plaisir de France*. A defender of obsolete luxuries and conceits, this magazine of style—sometimes quaintly academic but always a fierce partisan of great French traditions—has become the object of a fervent but highly personal cult among baby boomers now coming reluctantly into their full maturity. Showing them one of those color-saturated gravure plates on now-yellowing pages is like giving Proust five minutes alone with his mother's perfume bottle and a Q-Tip.

Old copies bring to life those afternoons spent leafing through glossies, intercepting them on their way to the attic. *Plaisir de France* is

where this generation of larval esthetes developed their fetishes for faille and pekin silk, for magical rooms full of things and materials now forgotten but once for sale at bygone stores in colors and prints that have also long since faded into oblivion. The Directoire or English mahogany formal dining room suites set against nineteenth-century landscape wallpaper—they still beckon, as do those bedrooms with heavy wooden beds, striped fabric on the walls, and net curtains on the windows; living rooms in eau-de-Nile; painted libraries with petit-point tapestries. To brighten things up, there were modern plaster sculptures and up-to-date Sèvres, straw and raffia, shells and Murano glass, painted panels and wrought iron.

In these pages, the old "reactionary elements" and artiste-decorators—those whom the worshippers of modernism swept under the rug—still reign. Or, rather, they were freeze-dried so that a new generation could bring them back to life at the right moment. Today, their roster has taken on a totemic cadence like a law firm out of Balzac: Arbus, Jean-Charles Moreux, Poillerat, Serge Roche & Pascaud.

These were the sure-handed eclectics who dared to suggest a return to the classical proportions of Palladio, Gabriel, and Ledoux, whom the

SANYAS & POPOT (AND OTHER PROUSTIAN POSTWAR MOMENTS)

Nostalgia is taken to pyrotechnic extremes.

modernists, in their haste, had brazenly cast aside like so many paper cups. And fifty years before they were needed, they provided answers for a generation to whom discovery would amount to rediscovery, for whom visual anthologies—elements cut, pasted, spliced, and compiled—would be a repository of hundreds of years of tradition or at least a practical way to gather up the threads.

The erudite allusions that came naturally to the likes of Jean Cocteau and Bébé Bérard stand in sharp contrast to the brash and fuzzy-minded eye candy of the Post-Modernists. These two men were giants of a colorful era that also belonged to a group of English eccentrics—Edward James, Stephen Tennant, and Oliver Messel. Those three names, once vaguely recognized for their gin-and-tonicy penchant for ornament, have now been catapulted into the first tier as major design references.

These rediscoveries are in part responsible for today's proliferation of plain walls—the better to show off that entrancing little 1937 witch portrait by Leonor Fini, the tiny gouache by Jean Hugo, the sacred-cow ceramic by Picasso, that Eugene Berman ink wash of Aïda, or dark watercolor by Tchelitchev. The furniture is in general rather light, sometimes painted, and preferably stamped Jansen (just like at the Windsors'): What could go more agreeably with a wrought-iron table and a Venetian mirror than a few objets de vertu and a glorious armchair? A dried clover from Louise de Vilmorin or a framed Reddish House rose signed by Cecil Beaton are ideal finishing touches in these interiors where nostalgia is taken to pyrotechnic extremes.

Devotees of Sanyas & Popot are known for their sense of correctness and authenticity. It's all too easy to joke about the way their plaster cravings sometimes get out of hand—the cabled columns, palm cornices, shell wall lamps, even curtains stiff under a layer of the stuff. But at their stubborn best, there is real authority in the way they are able to balance a magical modern object with the refined absolute of an eighteenth-century table. And they are vigilant against the imitators, who are legion, and fly into rages when they see this fragile equilibrium being distorted: They are constantly unearthing new secret references, and with the skill of a Chinese general they elude the pontificating of the new conformists who have made the style popular and whose homage can kill.

Now that the real Sanyas & Popot is no more, its devotees have switched to other merchants: These can generally be found in advanced decrepitude in the back courtyards of the rue de Seine or the rue Guénégaud lamenting how they are victims of unscrupulous money men out to ruin them. But their very financial straits keep them always ahead of the trends. Fans also have their secret boutiques tucked away between the Tuilleries and the place Vendôme on the rue du Mont-Tabor, and their pilgrimage sites (e.g., a hideous fifties-classical facade by Moreux in Bologne); they weep bitterly for the destruction of the Royal Lieu, the forties dance hall on the rue des Italiens, and of the Caravelle bar off the Champs-Élysées. And they pray daily for the health of the blackamoors in Vogue-Regency hideaways in Pigalle and London.

Doctoral candidates of the future will no doubt write grant proposals to identify and classify various currents in Sanyas & Popot style. There is the Bérard-Pompadour strain, set in its ways but also flowing and graceful. Then there is the Bérard-Eugénie, more historically minded, but not turning up its nose at a marble statue by Carrier-Belleuse, or an Art Nouveau terra-cotta that would look at

home on the exterior of Printemps, or a turned-leg stool in 1900 powder-puff Louis XVI (which was, after all, the inspiration for Bérard—and for Dior as well, if the truth be told); timid and literary, this offshoot merits volumes of its own.

Decorative extremists to be sure, the Sanyas & Popot faithful find their true home in *Les Styles* by Philippe Jullian: It is a book that presciently was written for them.

Having worn out all the fashions and exhausted all the myths, there's nothing left for fin-de-siècle style bulimics but to throw themselves at the oaken feet of a Louis XIII sideboard and start all over again.

English-speaking readers will no doubt miss some of the allusions that have been secreted throughout this volume as in a game of Find the Truffles. And they will have a good excuse: Many French readers will miss them as well. But I suppose that is what happens when a writer decides there are no waters that can't be muddied just a bit more and no reference that can't benefit from an extra veil. At least that has been my approach (or indulgence) as I prepared this book, which a chain of unforeseen encounters with remarkable people has brought thousands of miles from the table on which it was written.

The poor bulimic style-hound mentioned in the closing lines is in fact an impious reference to a famous character from fin-de-siècle French literature, Des Esseintes, the hero of Joris-Karl Huysmans's novel *À Rebours*. He was, if you like, a poster boy for European decadence, someone who could make Oscar Wilde or Aubrey Beardsley blush. Equal parts perpetrator and victim of the systematic saturation of all the senses, a tireless pursuer of the most quiveringly vivid sensations, a lover of the most haunting perfumes and the rarest foods, Des Esseintes represents the epitome of artificial culture, the ne plus ultra of sophistication, and the unbridled hysterical search for new pleasures. But such a quest always carries with it the threat of being satiated: And when Des Esseintes reached his limit, he found he had only two choices—suicide or religion. As it happens, he chose the latter and dedicated the rest of his life to seeking out and venerating obscure medieval female saints.

We also live at a fin de siècle. The unquenchable thirst for modes and models that has characterized decor addicts in recent years makes Des Esseintes look like a dabbler. One of the things that inspired this book—in addition to a desire to immortalize the scenes of my adolescence and, as it turns out, Christian Lacroix's as well—was astonishment at the speed at which trends and currents have given way one to another over the last thirty years.

This attention-deficit voraciousness is the mark of the baby boomer generation, who are just now being dragged kicking and screaming into maturity. As the first generation of modern times not to have known war, they have made superfluous things their necessities. Crazed by invention, novelty, consumption, and curiosity about the work of decorators long since forgotten or

misunderstood in their own day, these baby boomers seemed to me, rightly or wrongly, to be approaching a state of exhaustion of Huysmanesque proportions by the time the recession of the early 1990s came along. I sensed that a kind of amnesty had been declared in the decor wars.

For evidence that my instincts were correct, I had to look no further than the shelter magazines that have recently been proliferating so wildly all over the planet. About two years ago they started proclaiming in unison the charms of the understated and the neutral—the virtues of measured classicism as seen through a haze of pale colors and natural materials, of furniture with simple primitive lines, of the good taste inherent in basics like white china, cotton, linen, and ecologically correct straw. I felt as if I were witnessing a battlefield through clearing smoke.

Of course the stylistic rogues' gallery I have assembled here is by no means exhaustive. And while I make no apologies for either its biases or omissions, I can easily think of some things I could have added.

One is the Primary Colors school being tirelessly promoted by a certain decoratrix in England. Its blues, reds, greens, and yellows are so plain and determined, the motifs so calculatedly clumsy, the ceramics so thick and glossy that one must assume she was frightened by a Matisse collage as a child. A three-dimensional advertisement for the glories of acrylics, this style is enough to make the color-blind grateful for their condition. To the chant of "Down with subtlety and all its wiles," these rooms use a strident cheerfulness to chase away all blues but their own. Maybe only the sun-starved British could embrace such unrelenting brightness.

Another modern trend whose gory details I have spared my readers comes from the other side of the Channel, where it is shamelessly promoted by a certain French shelter magazine. This is the Childish Tinkering school of decoration whose adherents seem hypnotized by a compulsion for salvage: Looking at their homes, one would think the town dump was the most desirable possible provenance. This style is the far side of Shabby Chic in its passion for decay and recycling and its devotion to slapdash paint and sloppy workmanship in all things. The promiscuous do-it-yourselfers who have perfected it—if that is the right word. They have let their waste-not ideology freeze them in a state of perpetual adolescence.

American decoration, it seems to me, is caught between two extremes. On the one hand there is the slightly loopy but irresistible eclecticism of a Rose Cumming, the New York decorator of the forties and fifties who had a passion for chiffon and silver-leaf walls. The phantasmagorical creations of the Los Angeles designer Tony Duquette take this tendency almost to the level of Outsider Art for the inside. Nothing seems to frighten decorators of this persuasion as they patch together their wild and frequently wonderful collages of looks, periods, and materials. In a way, Liberace was the perfect master of this archi-rococo: By the time the architect Robert Venturi wrote his famous book *Learning from Las Vegas*, Liberace already had his Ph.D. in the subject.

At the other extreme, there is the new and somewhat febrile minimalism that is the specialty of a famous New York fashion designer in whose recently constructed store framed black-and-white photographs stand out as splashes of color. It is a glorious mosaic of political correctness and WASP's Last Stand, where the natural and perfectly plain become the last word in sophistication. Its portion-controlled reticence is yet another step toward the global homogenization of design—the "world car" approach to style carefully calibrated to appeal to the New World and the Old, to New York and Milan, to London and Paris. It's the opening chapter of the End of History.

And it leads us back to our starting point. If the nineteenth-century Des Esseintes swooned over fragrant lilies and vapors of opium, the twentieth-century ones withdraw into their universe of natural stone, frosted glass, and muted pastels where the greatest fear is of offending anyone.

At the start of this note I mentioned a chain of unforeseen encounters with remarkable people. In the end, they are what cause books to be made: At least they were responsible for putting this album between covers. Among those people were Barrie McIntyre, a living encyclopedia of design to whom nothing remains hidden in this demanding discipline; Mitchell Owens, who brought the French edition to the attention of the public in lands across the sea; Christopher Phillips, who seemed to know just how to turn my impossible French into English; Eric Baker Design Associates, the book designers; Anne Yarowsky and Melissa Roberts of Simon & Schuster Editions, to whom this edition quite simply owes its existence.